I thank God for helping me this far.
Good company brightens our days. Thank you for being my companions.
I love you Z.T.L

JANAINA TEIXEIRA
2024

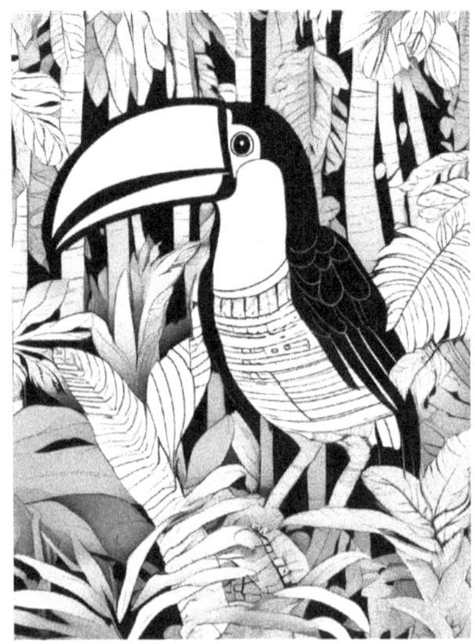

Write your name here

○─────────────────────────────────────○

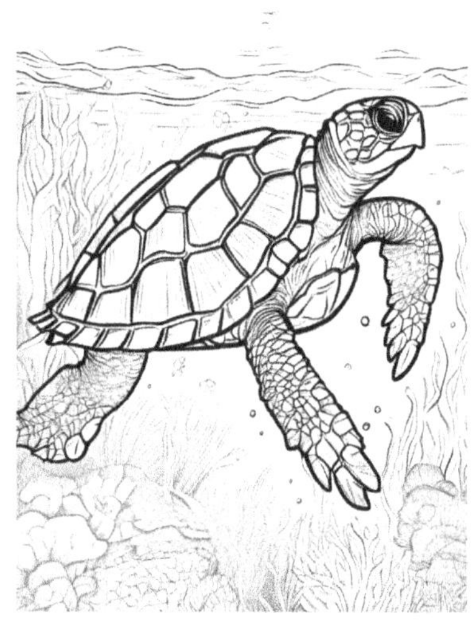

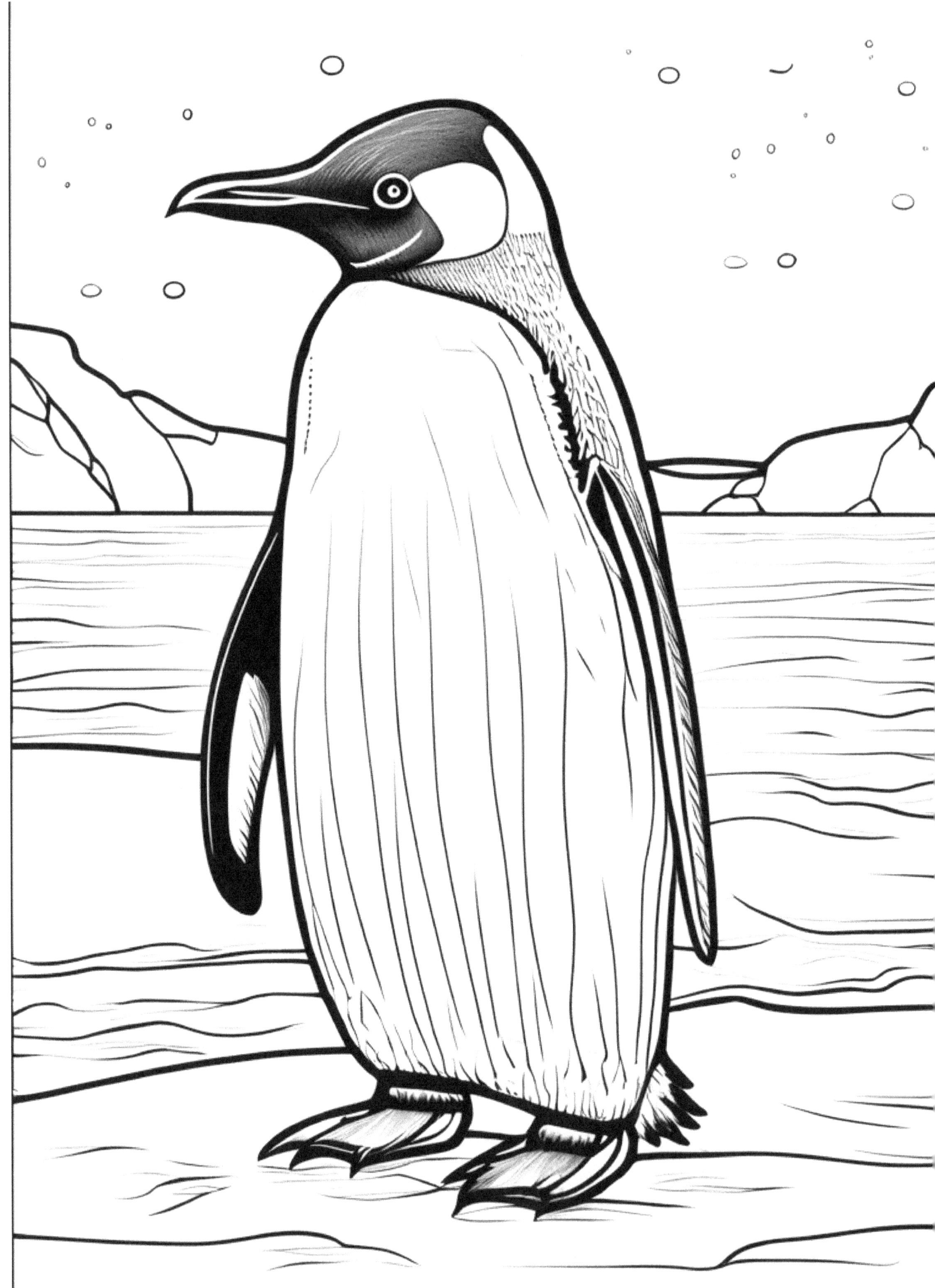

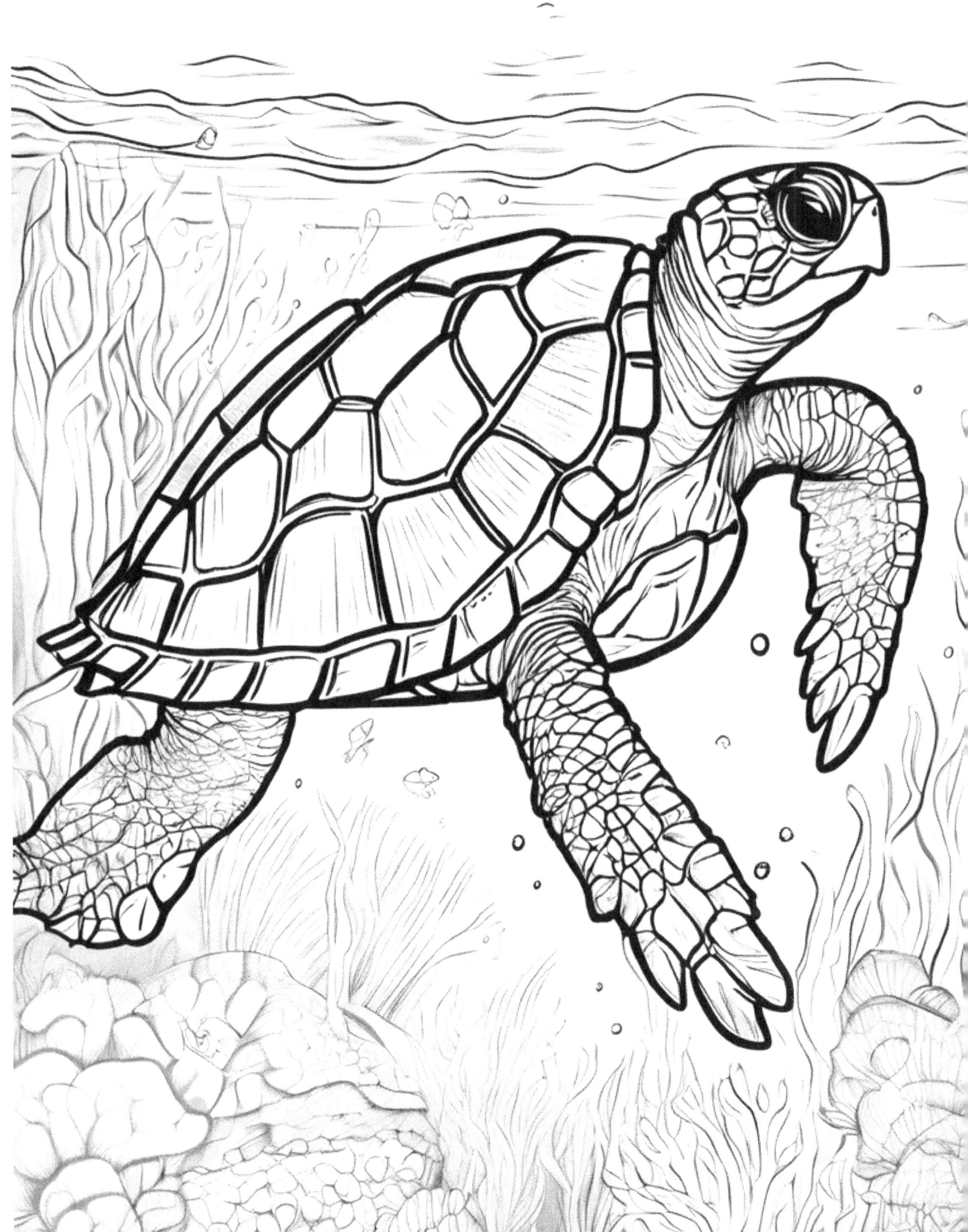

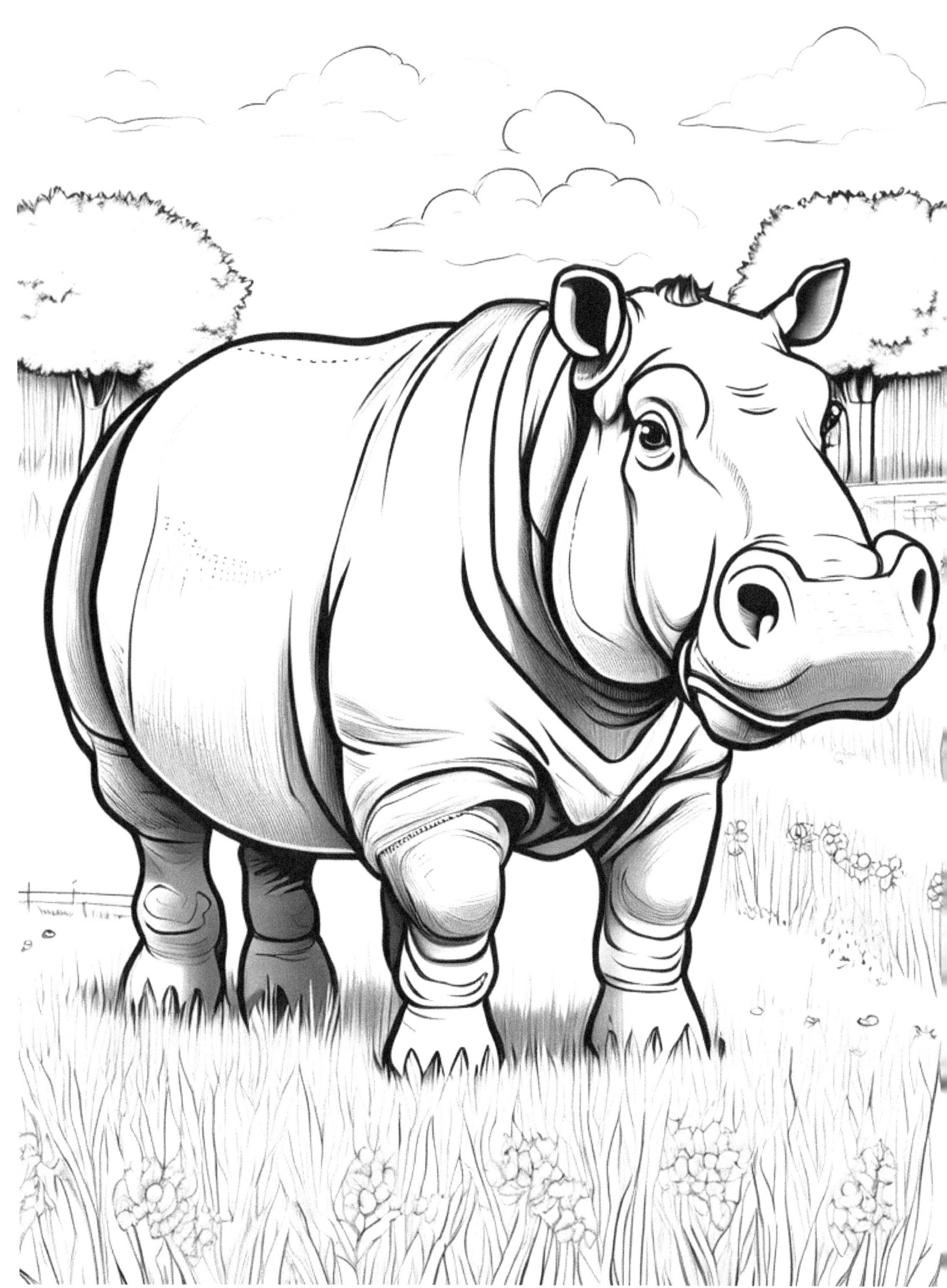

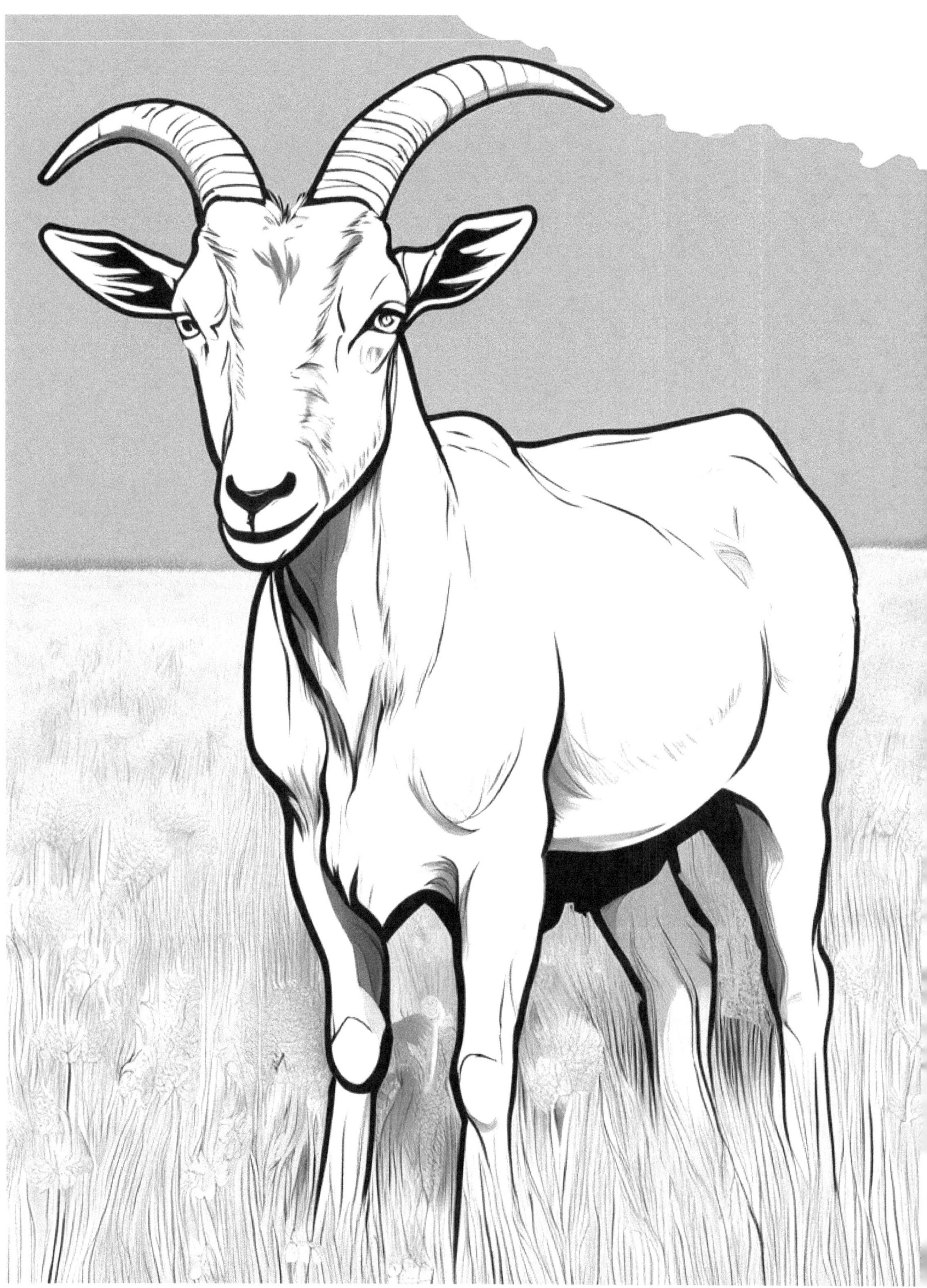

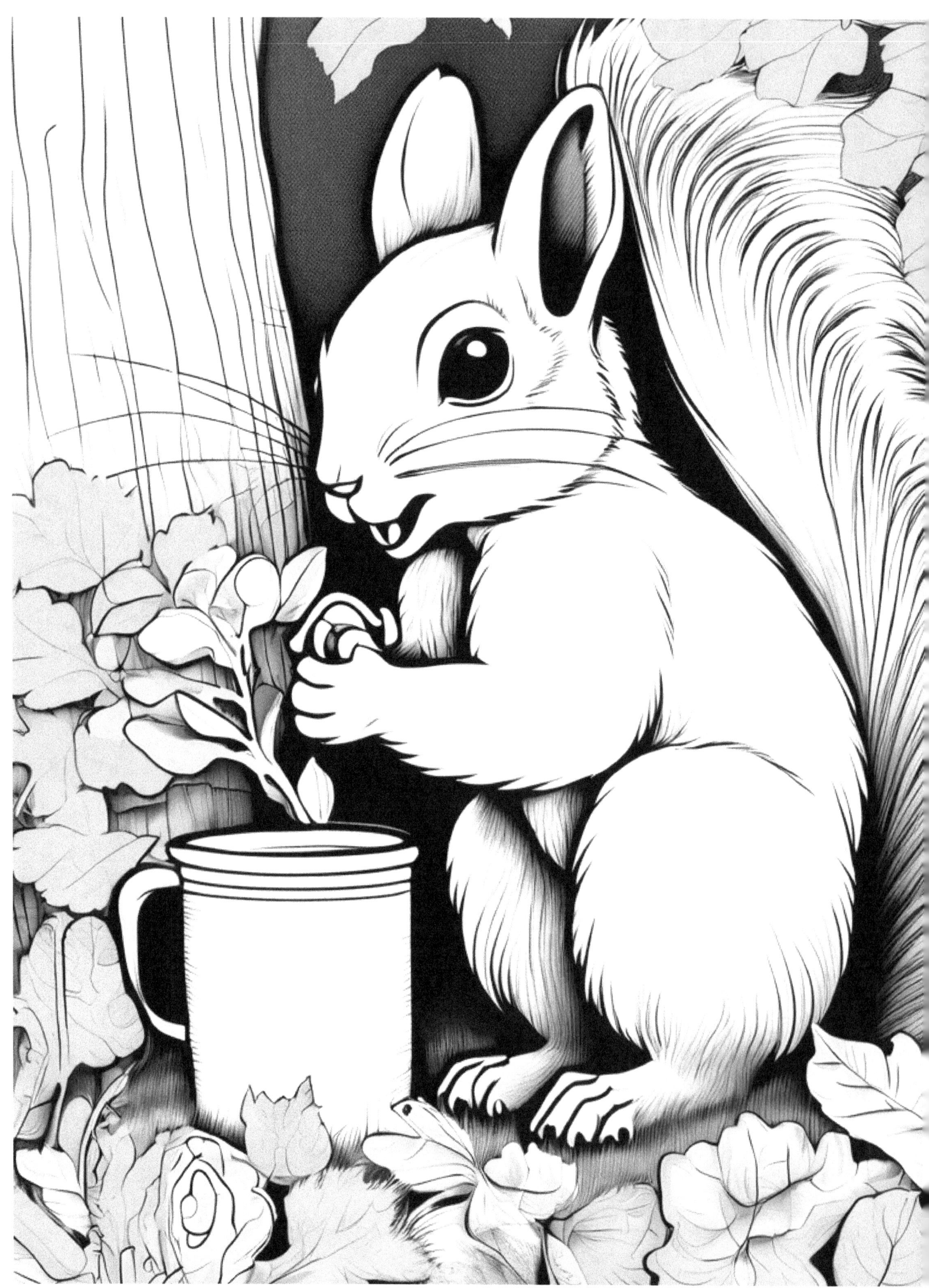

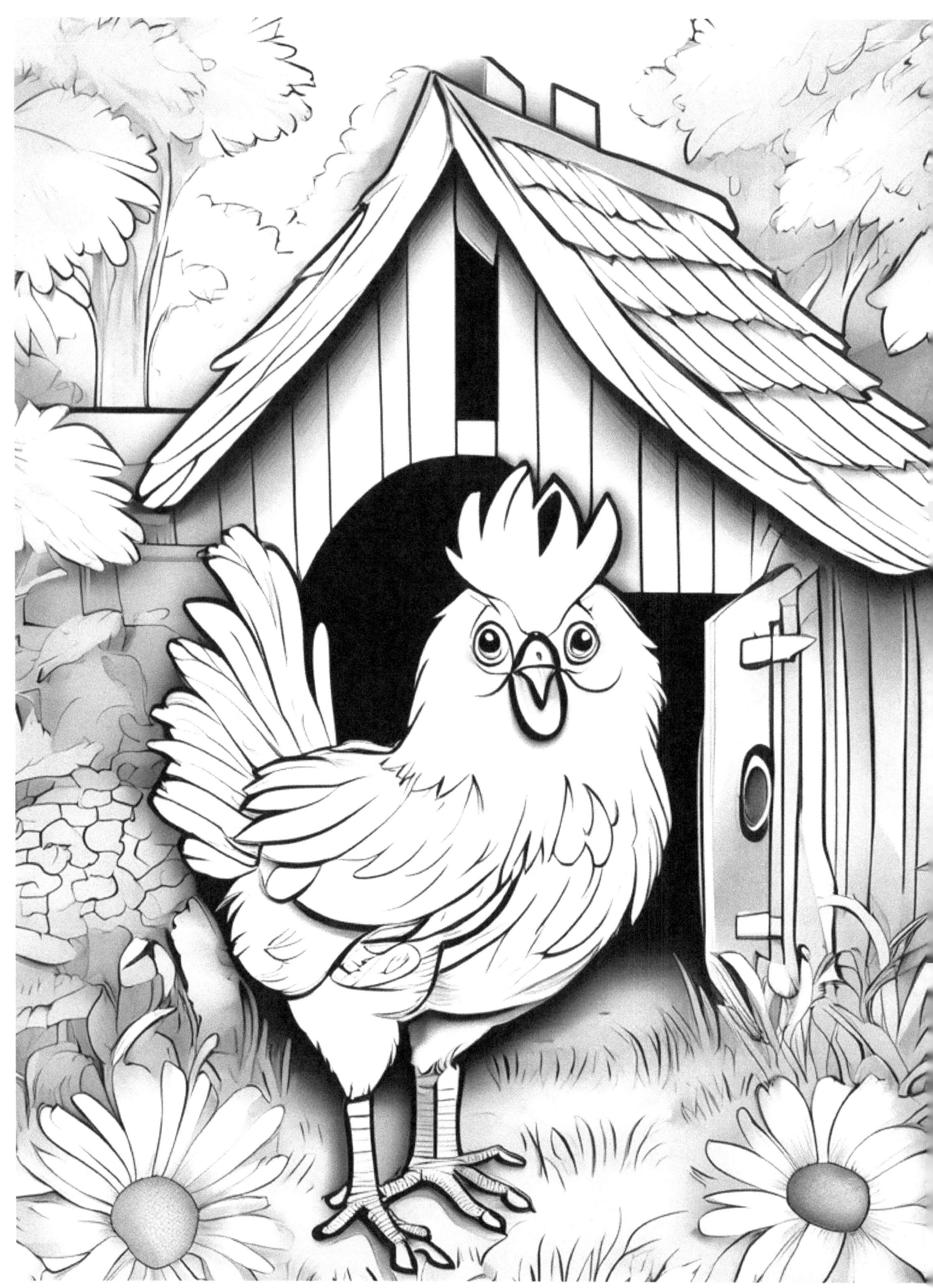

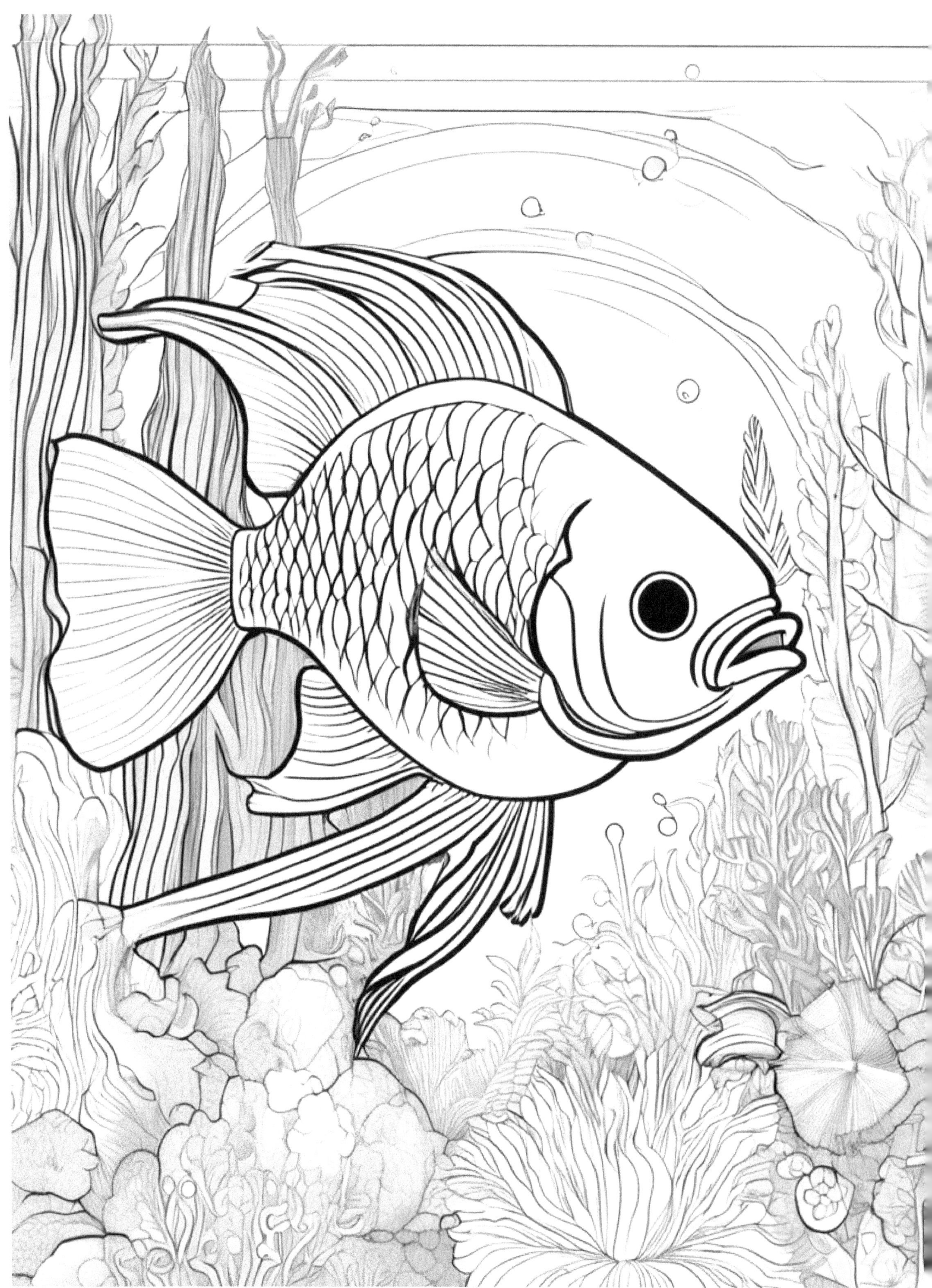

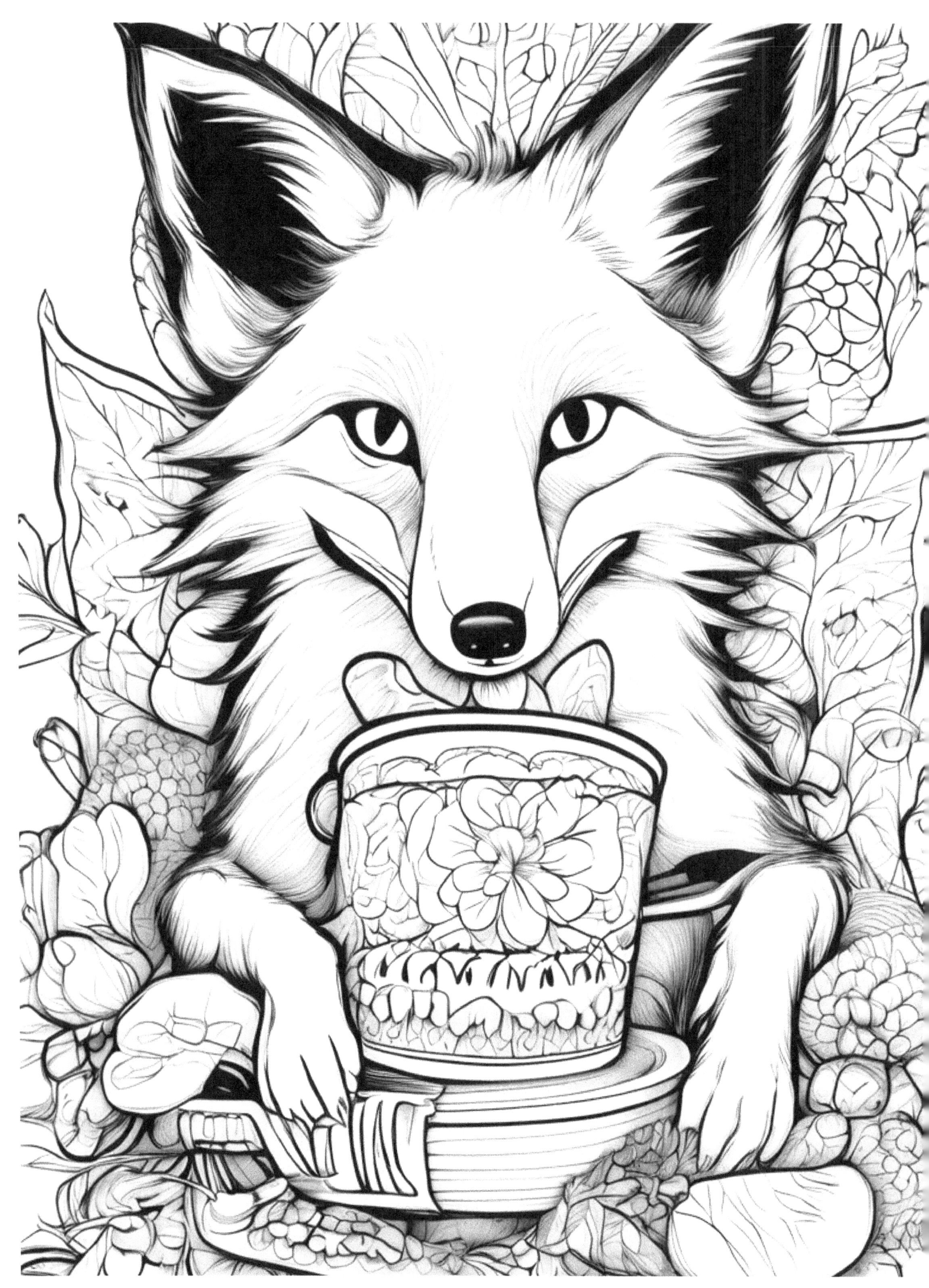

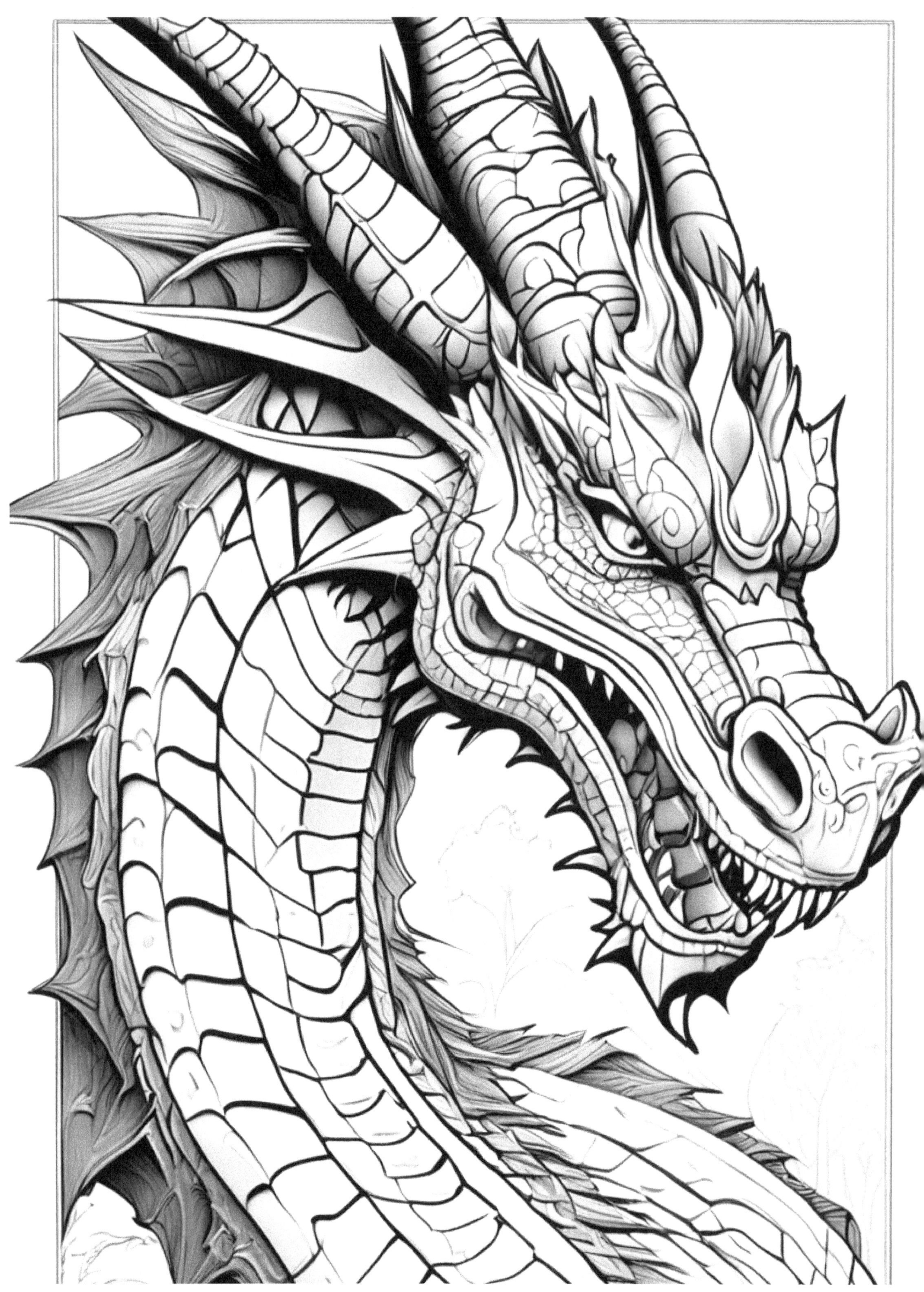

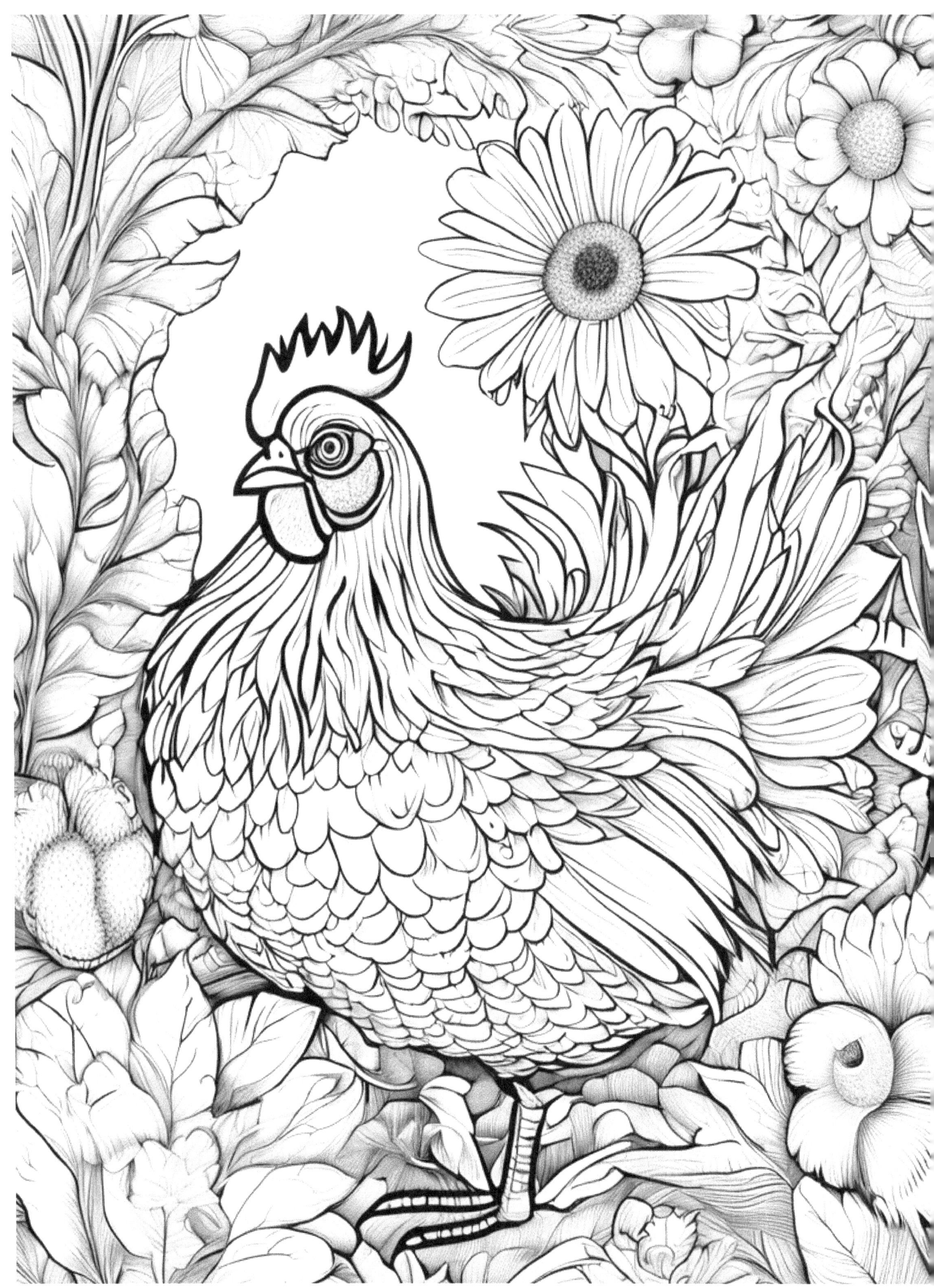

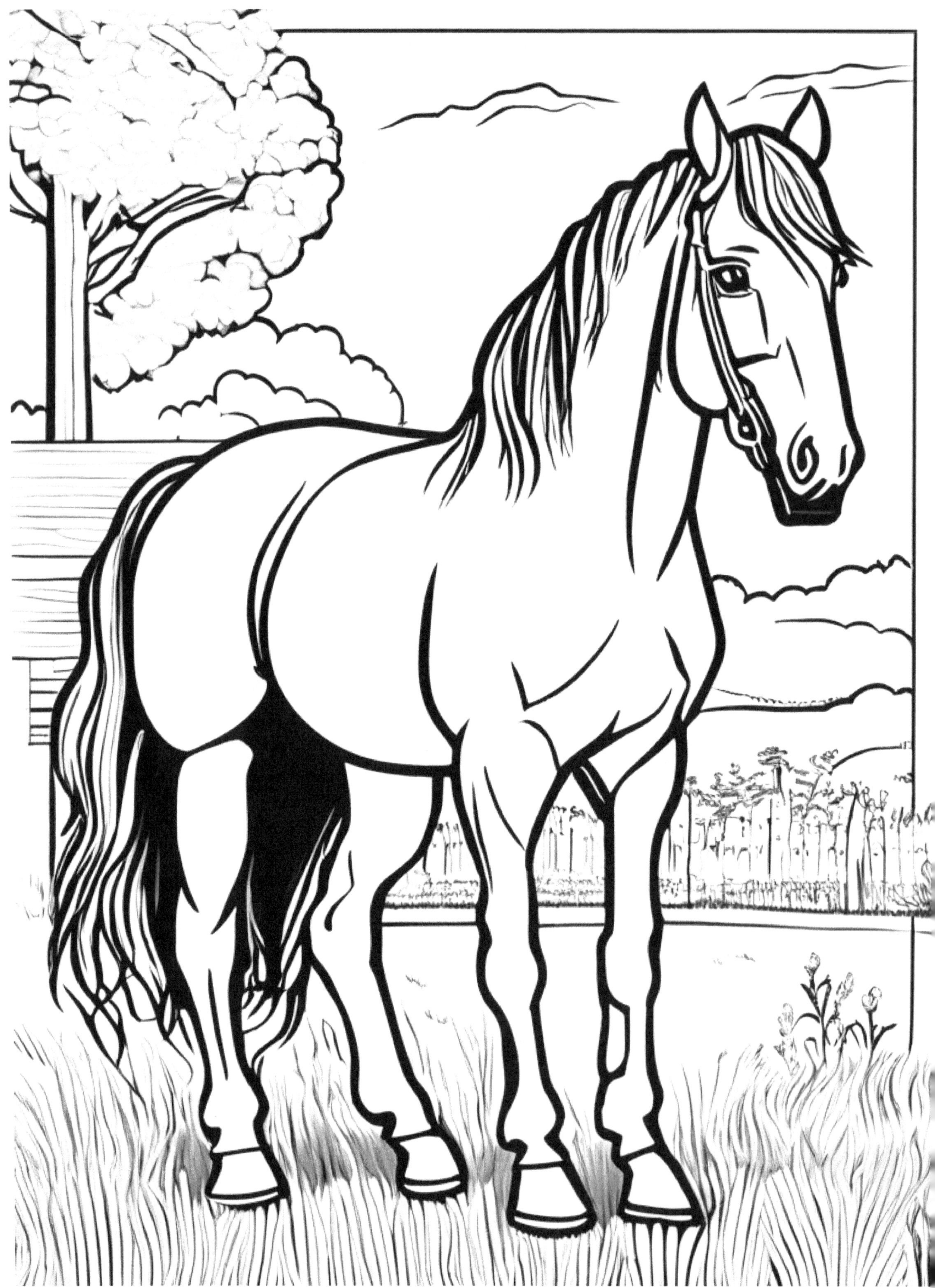

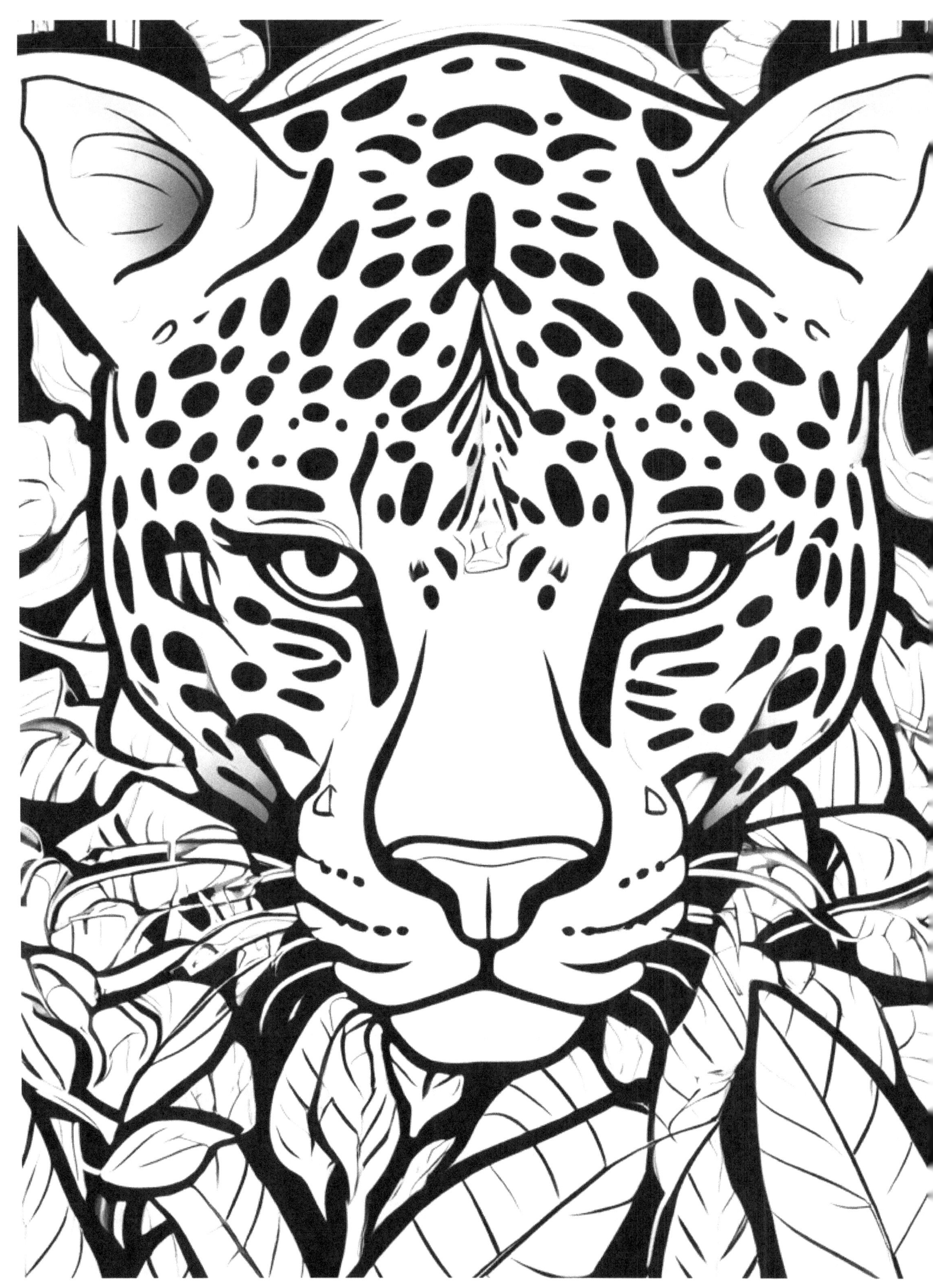

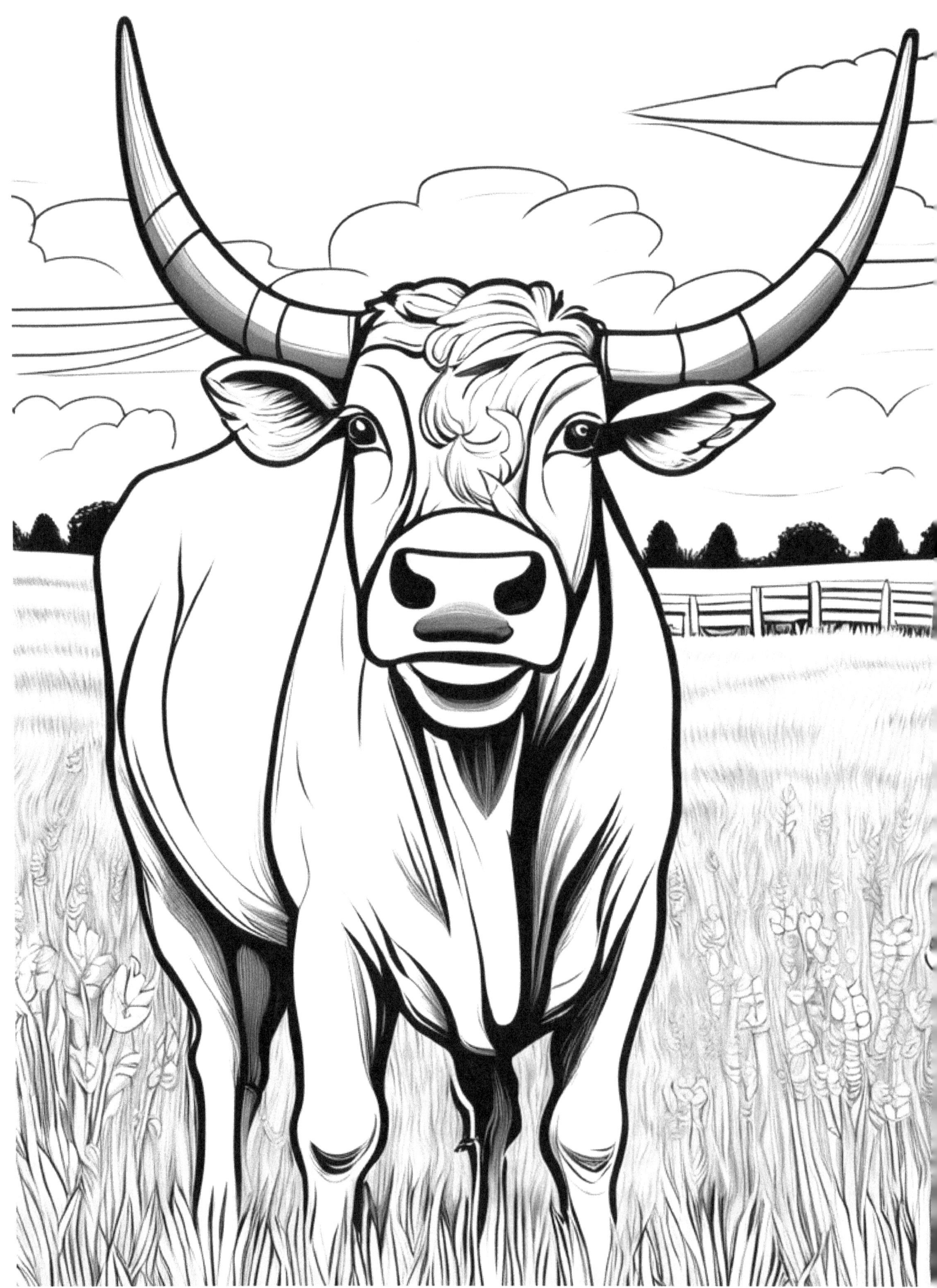

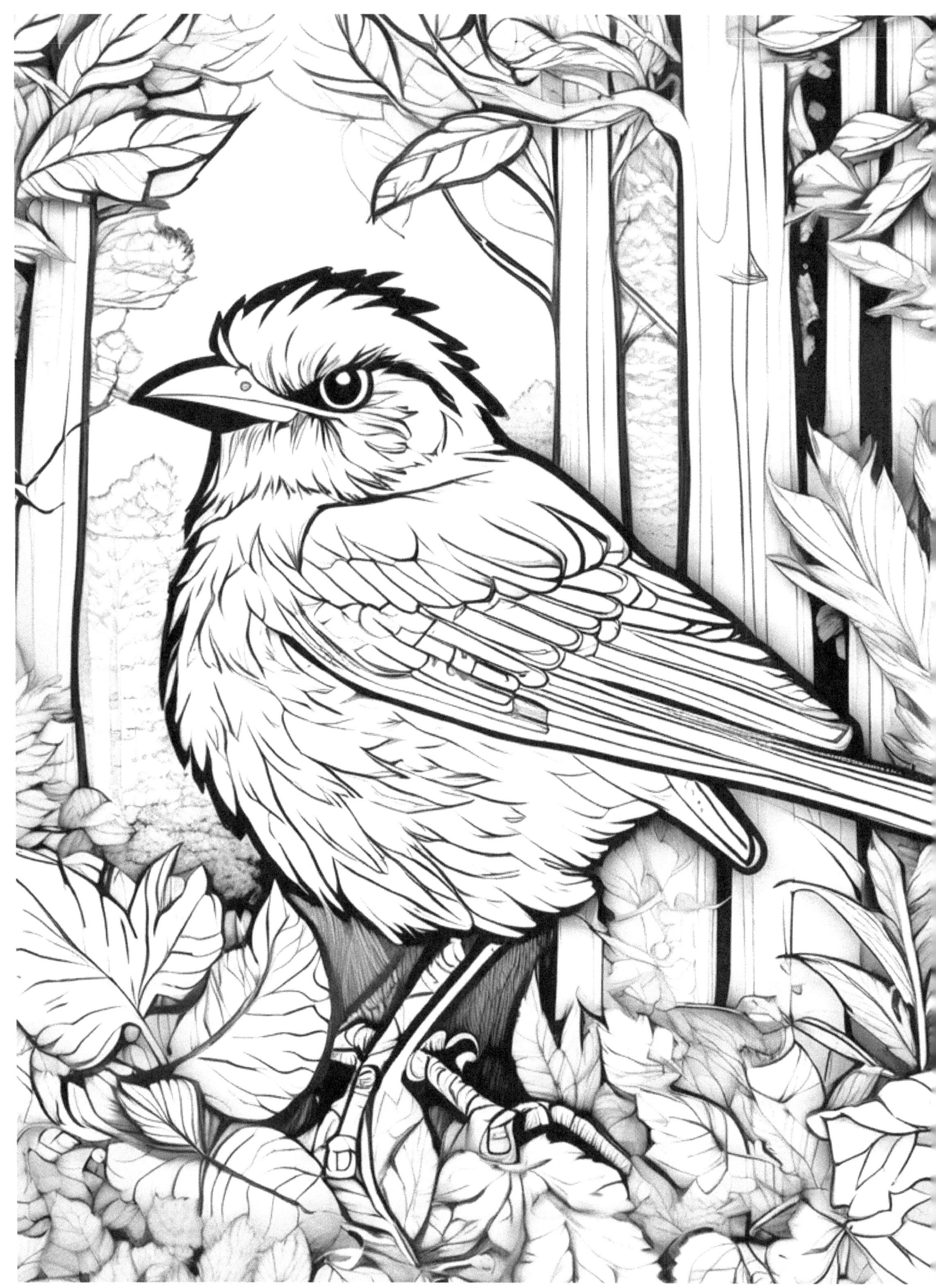

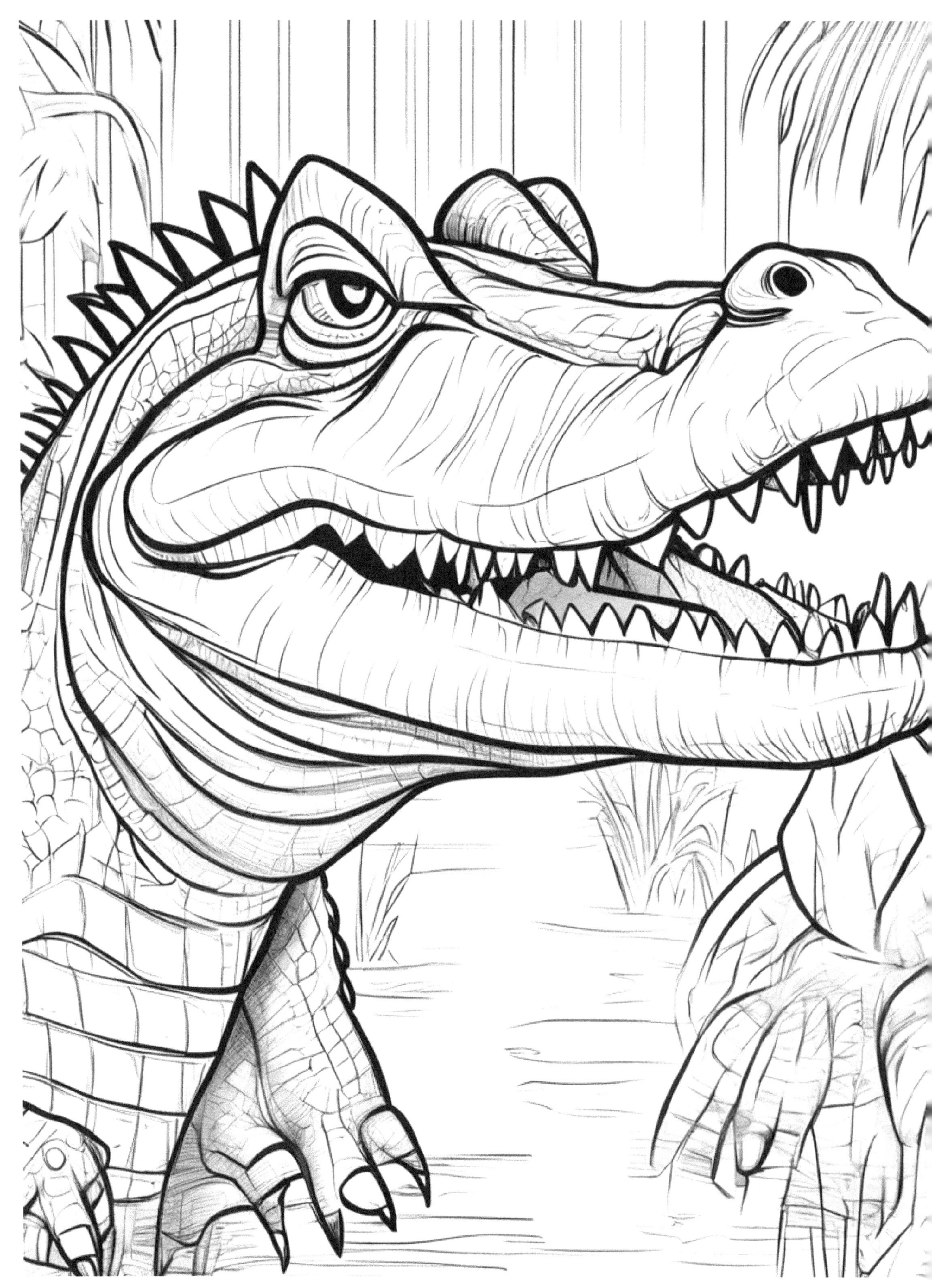

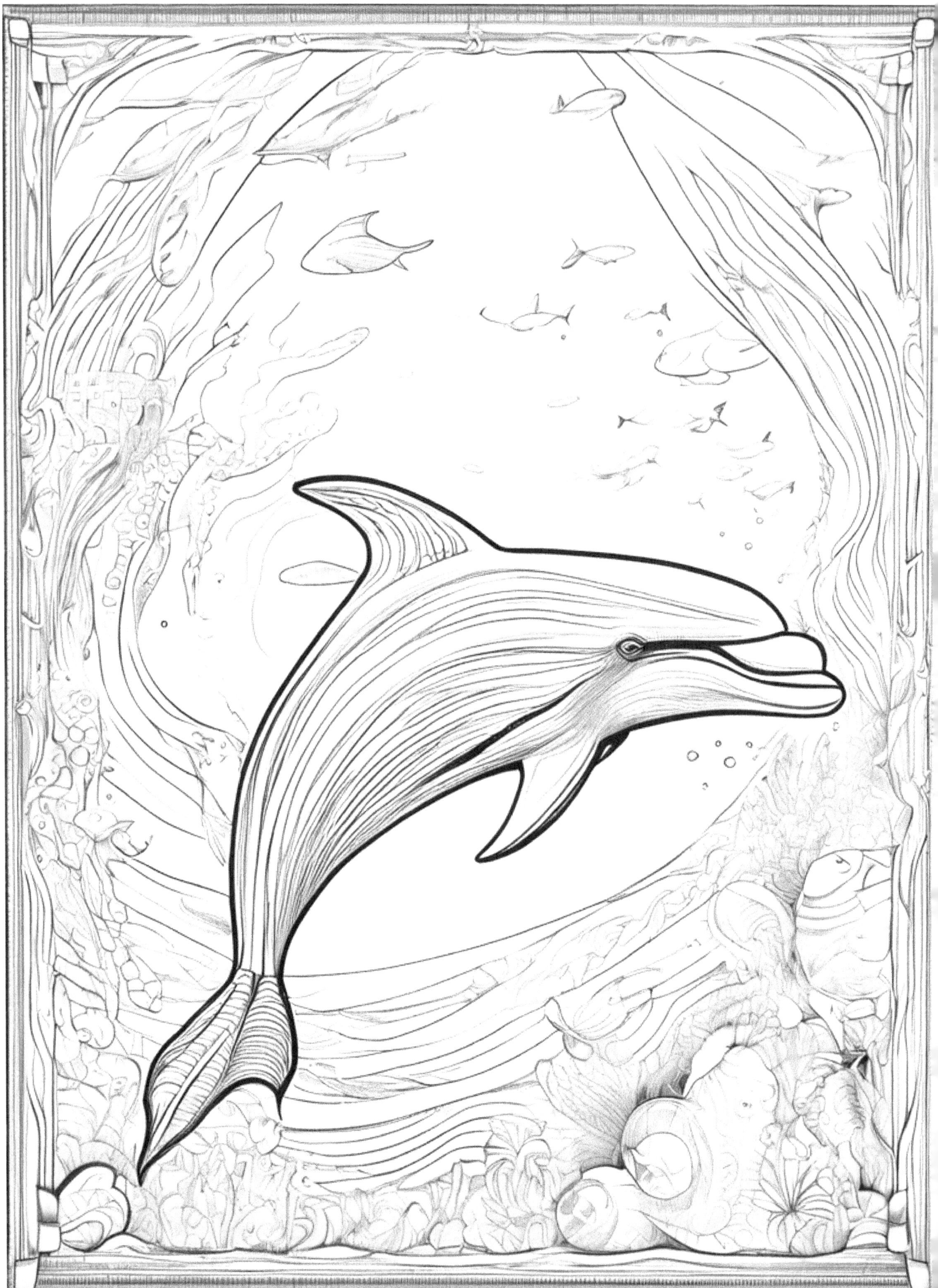

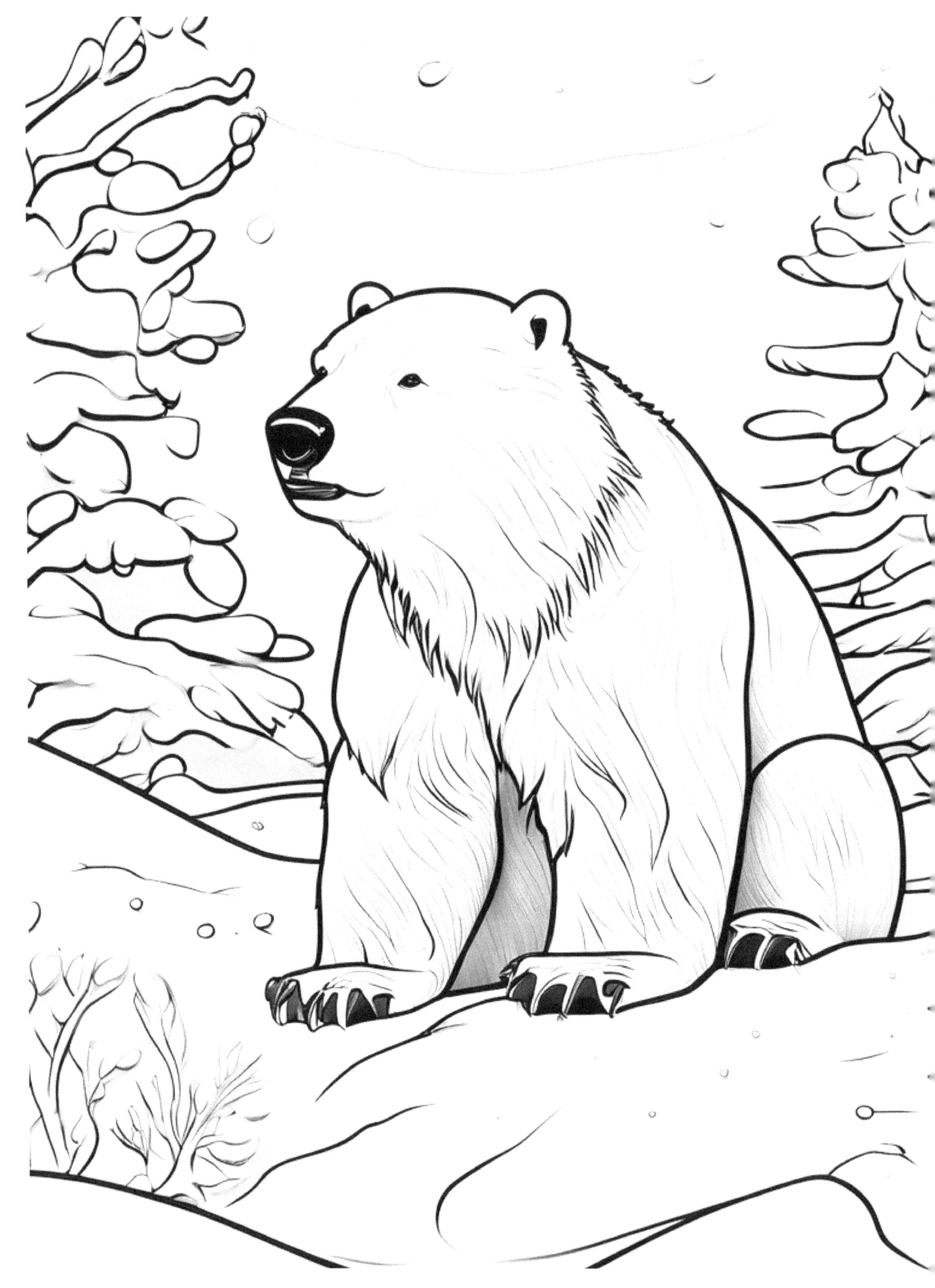

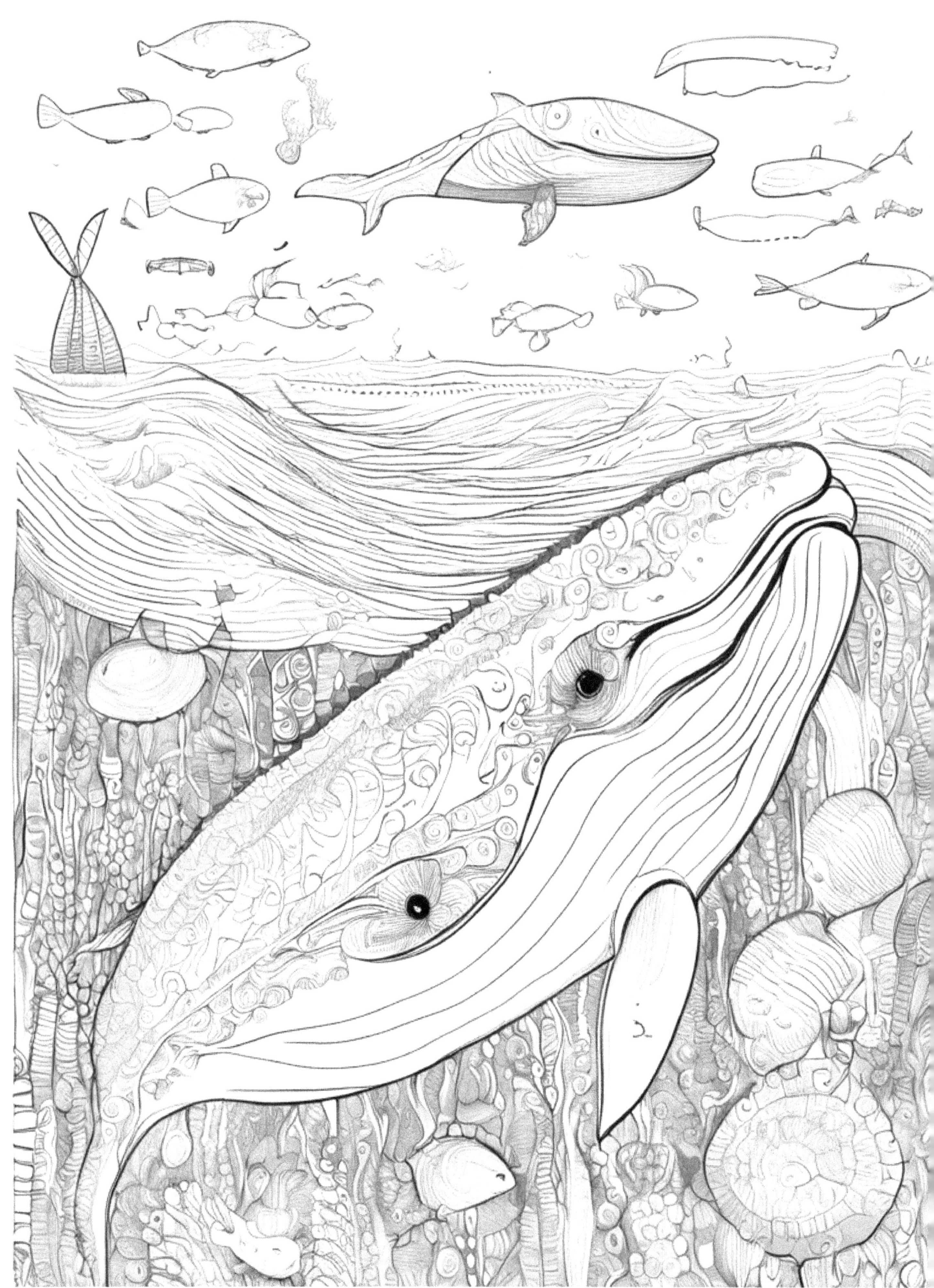

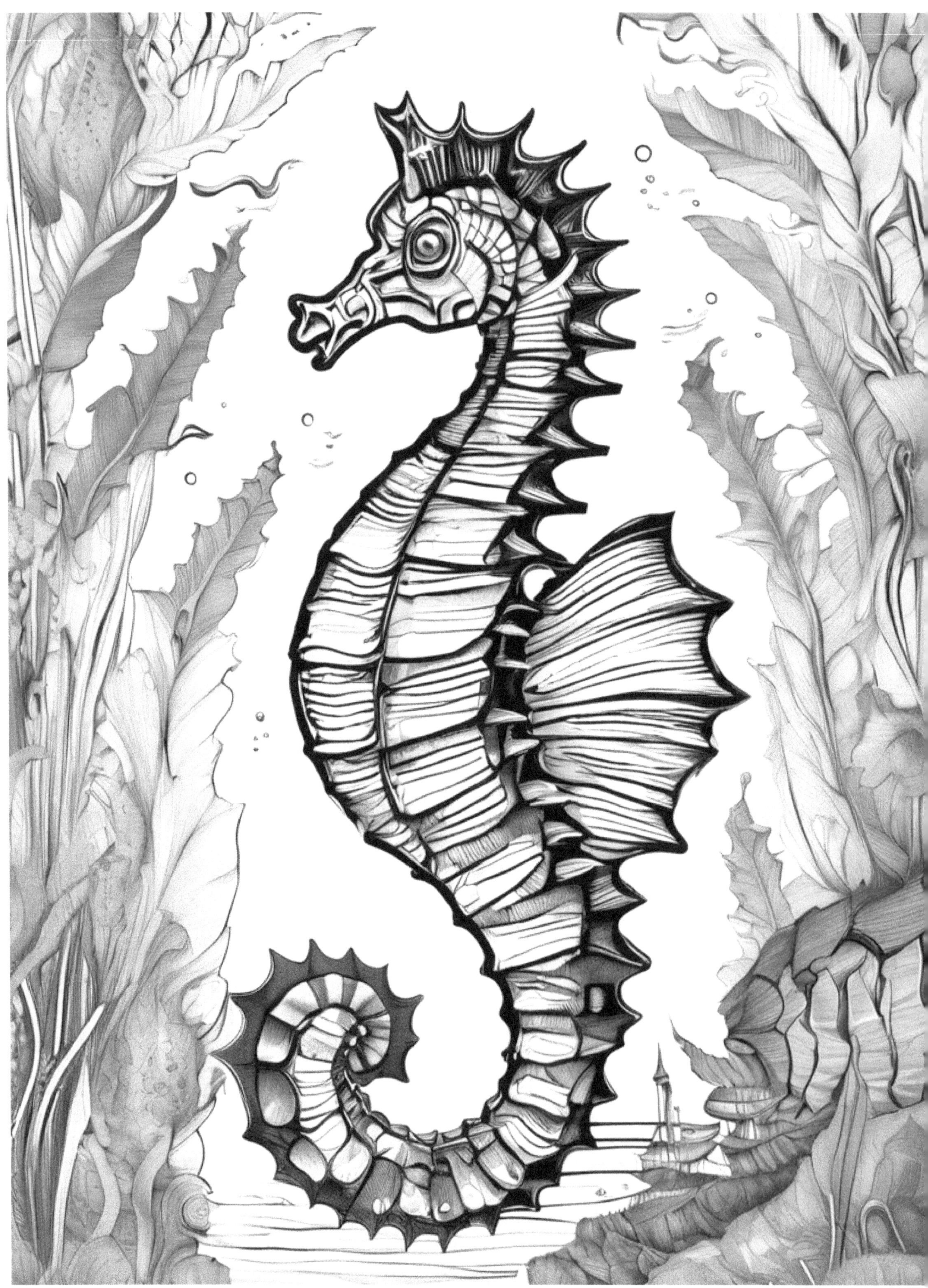

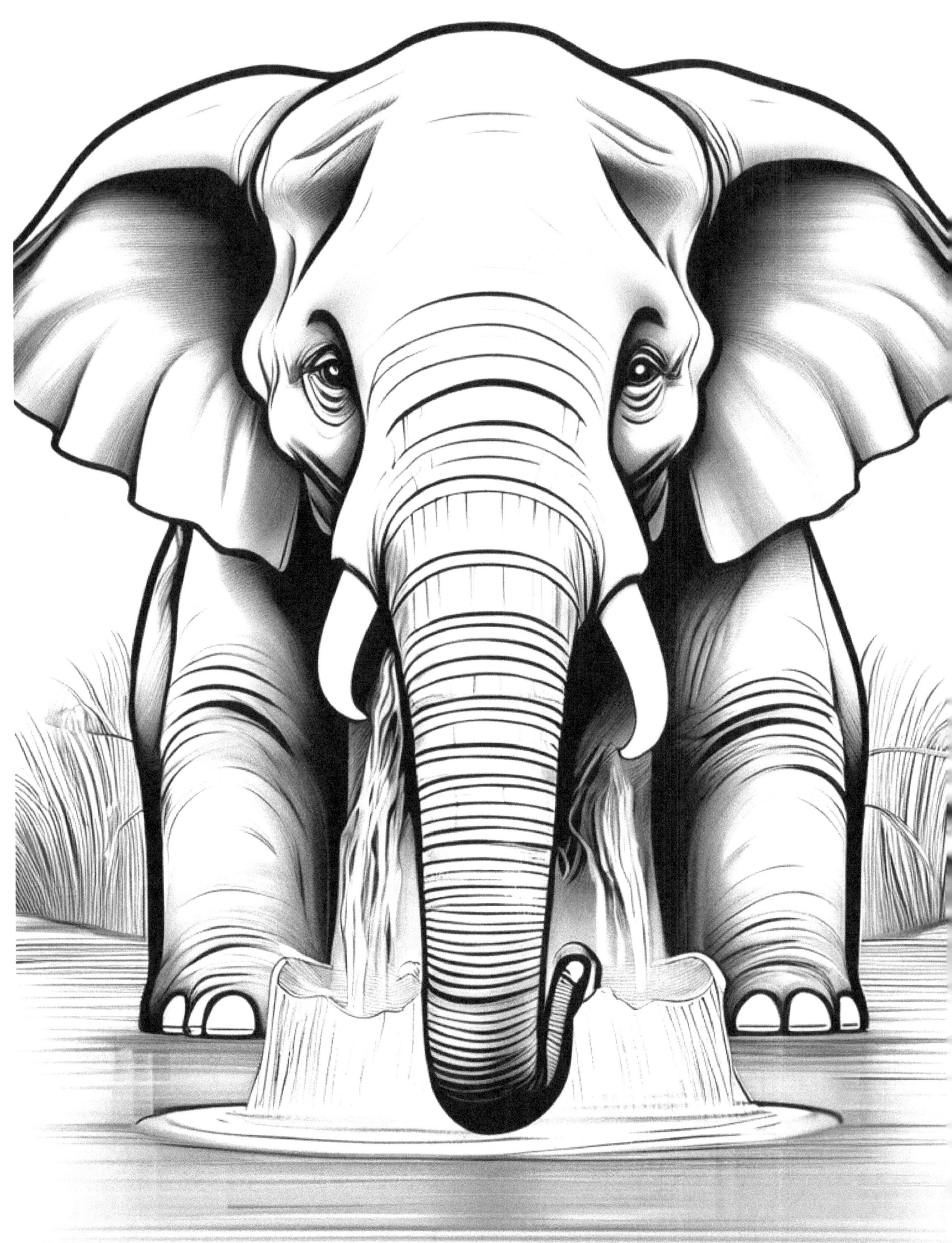

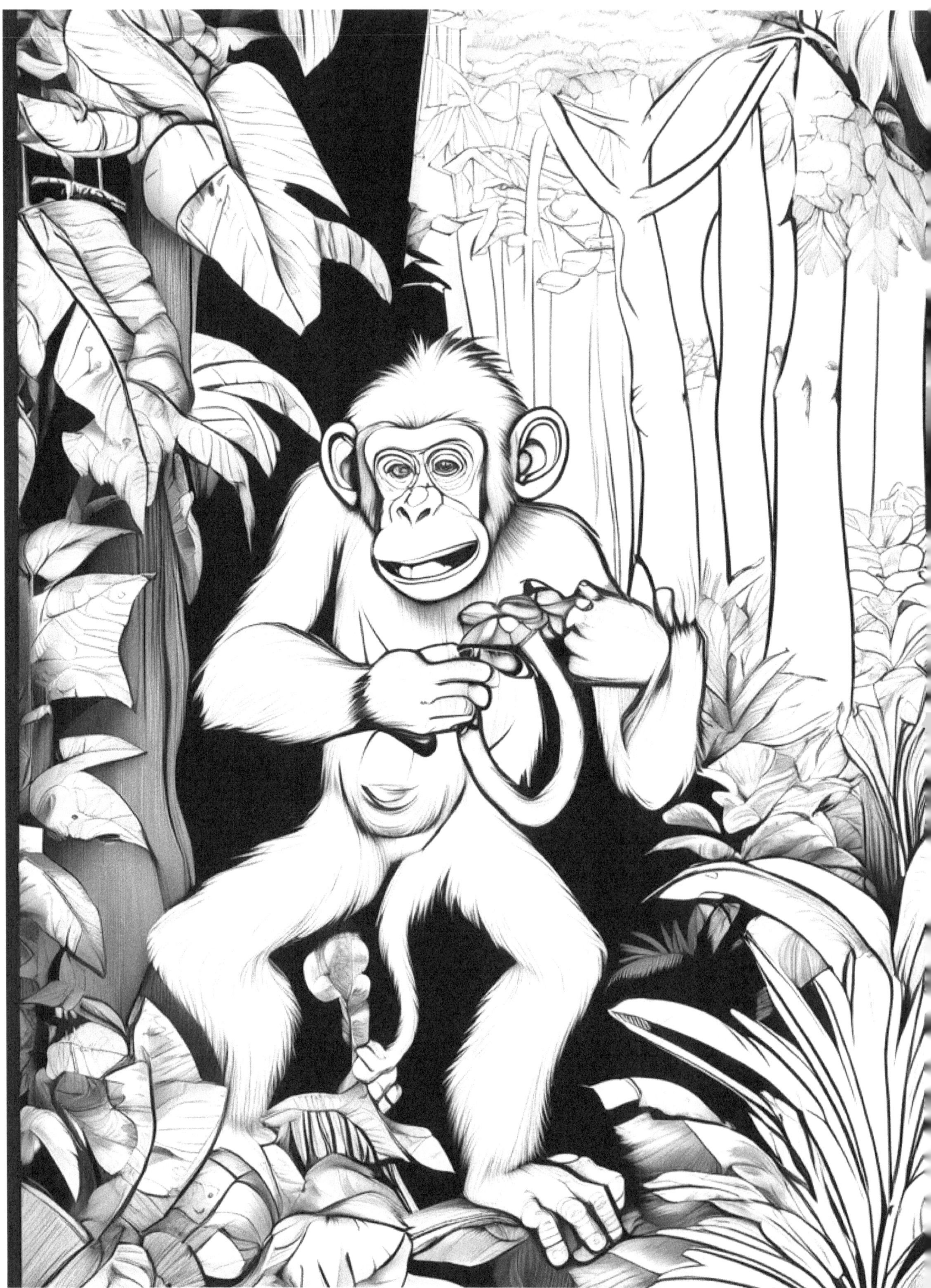

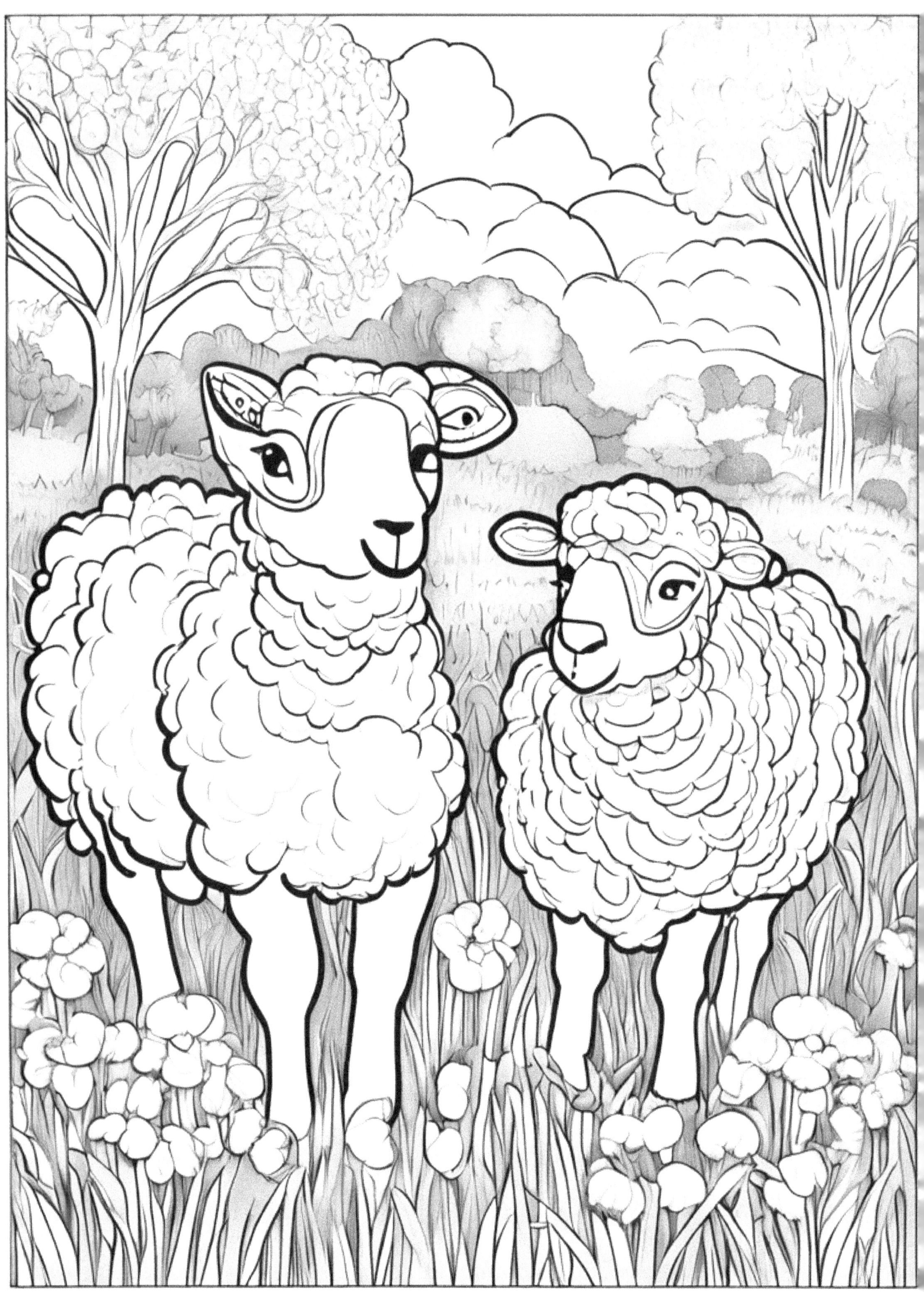

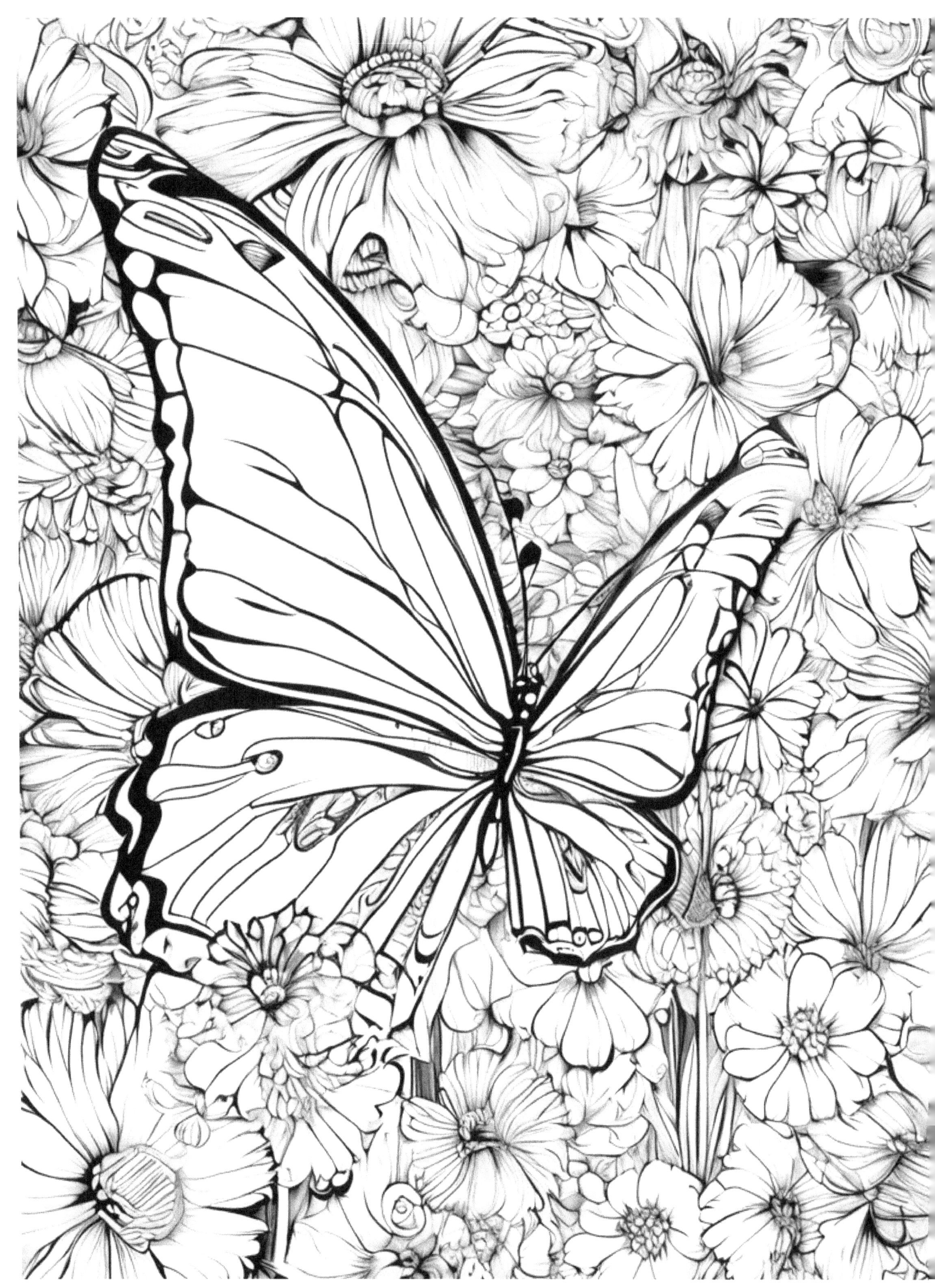

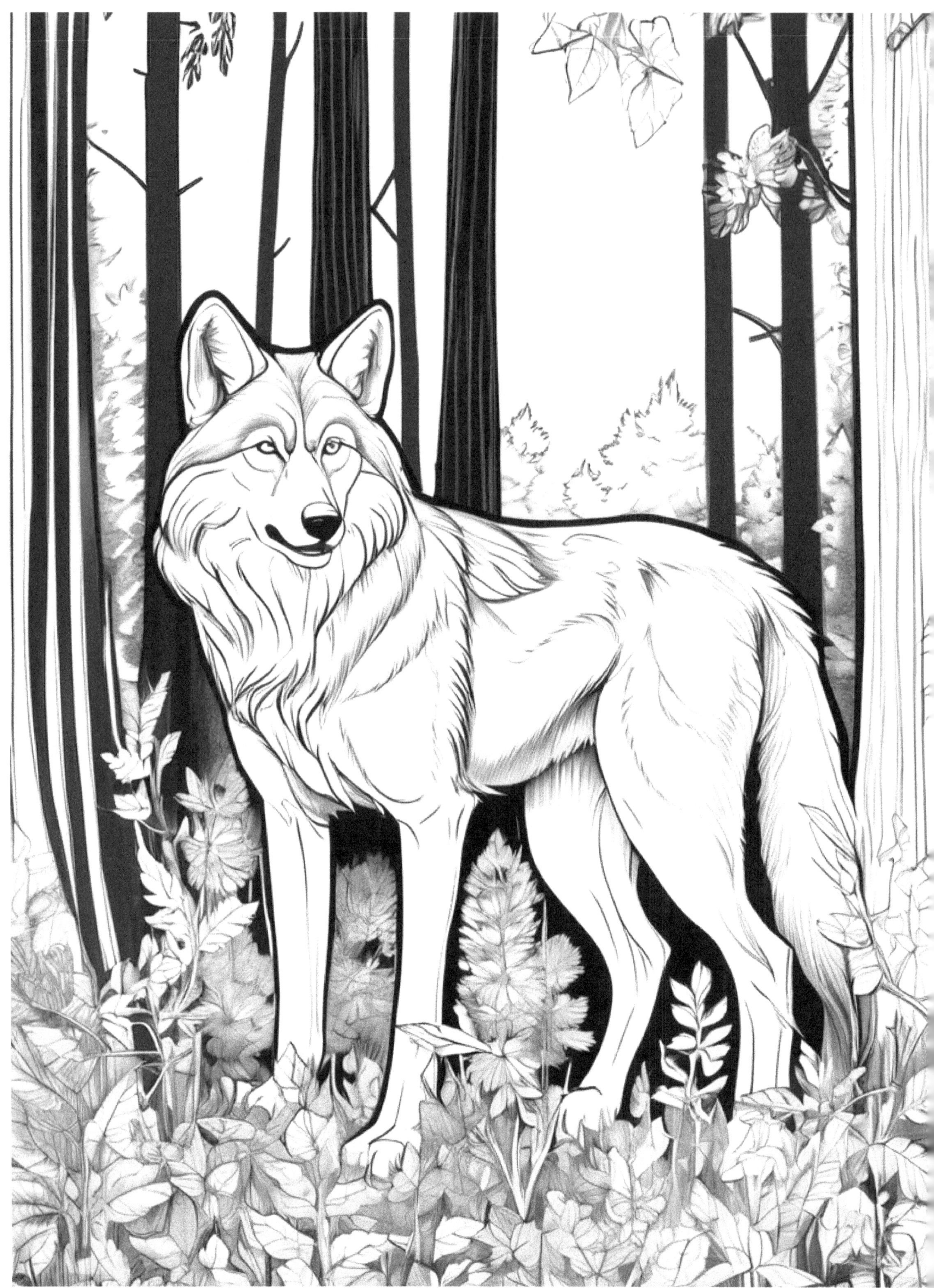

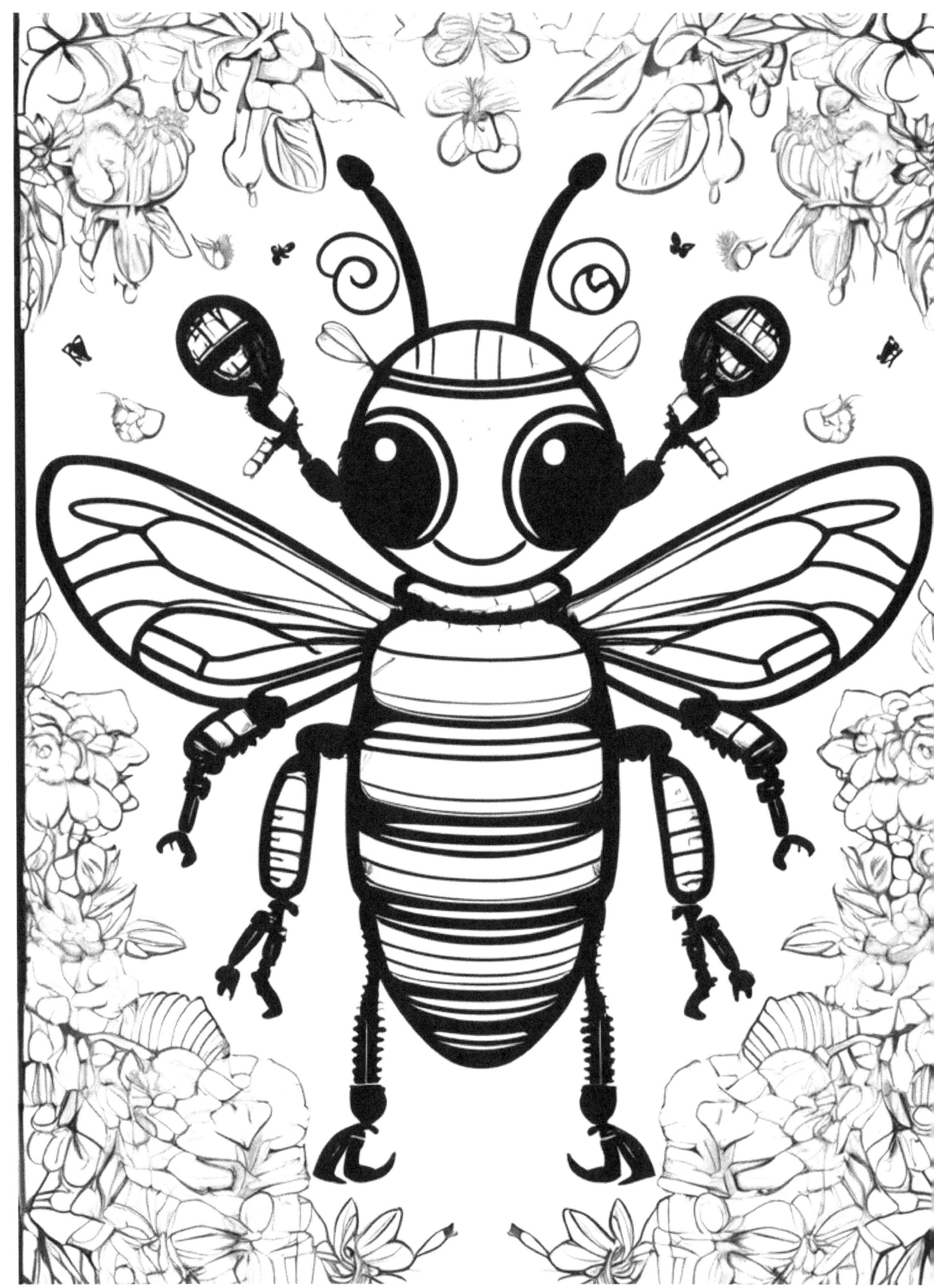

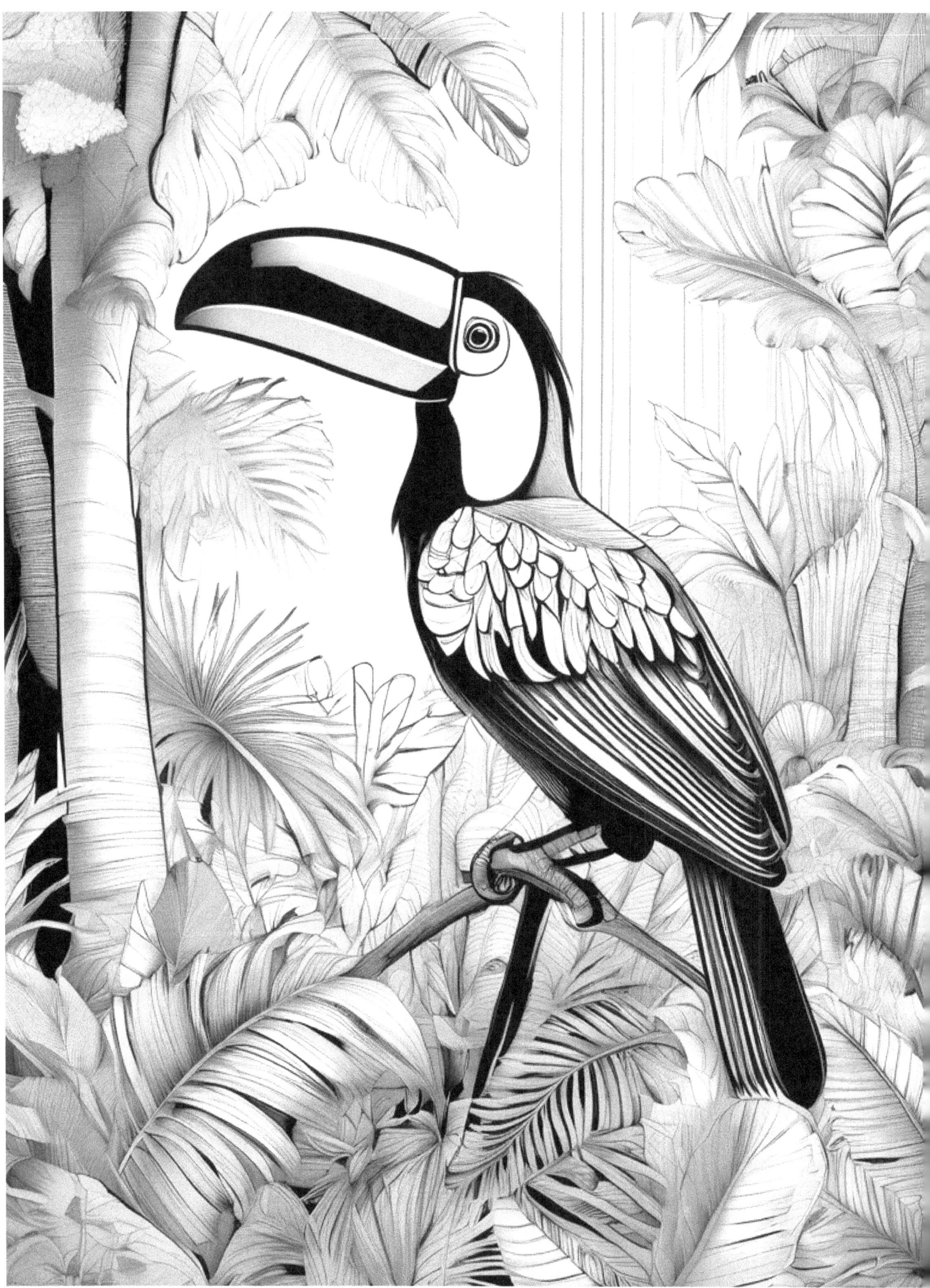

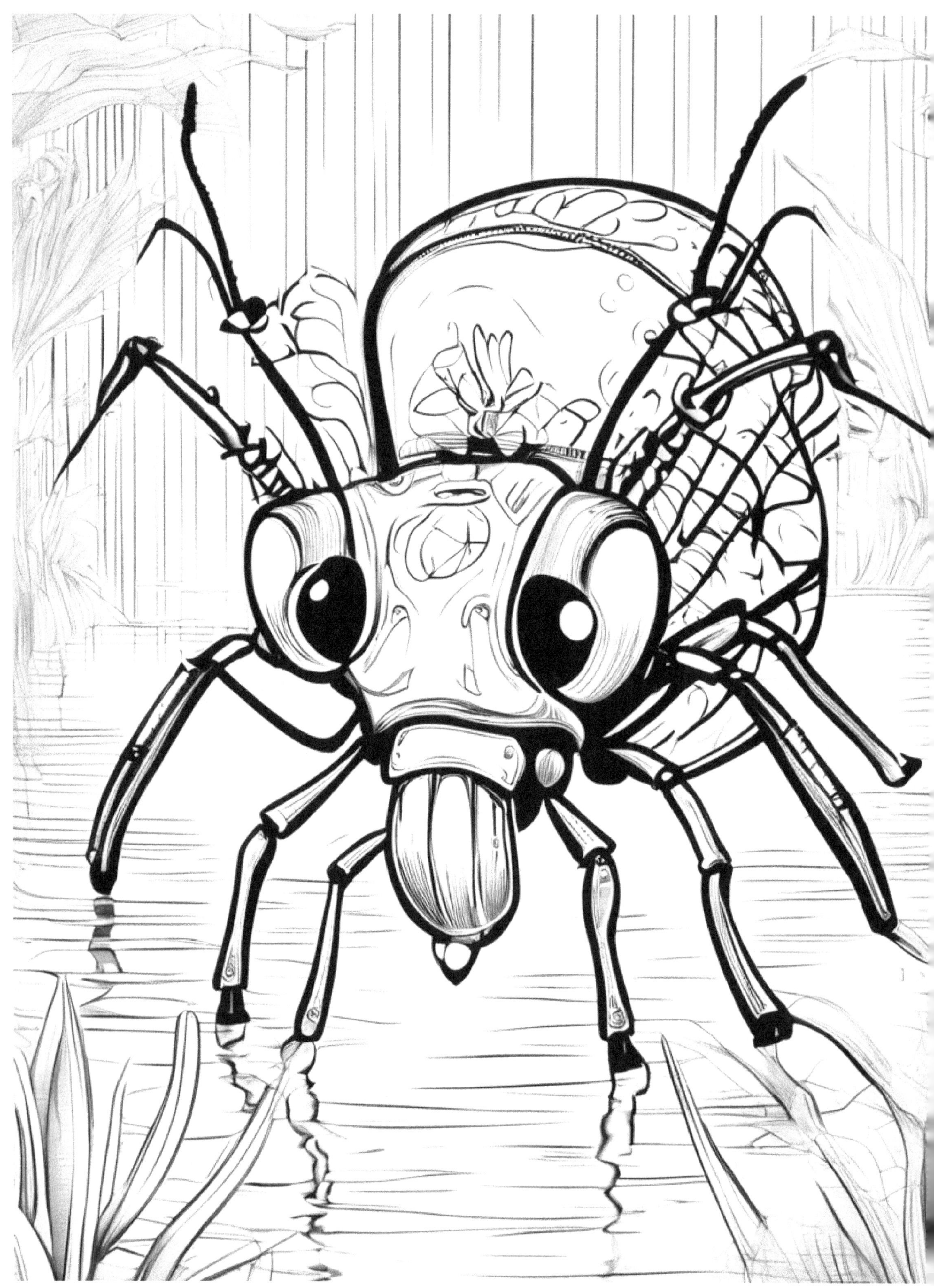

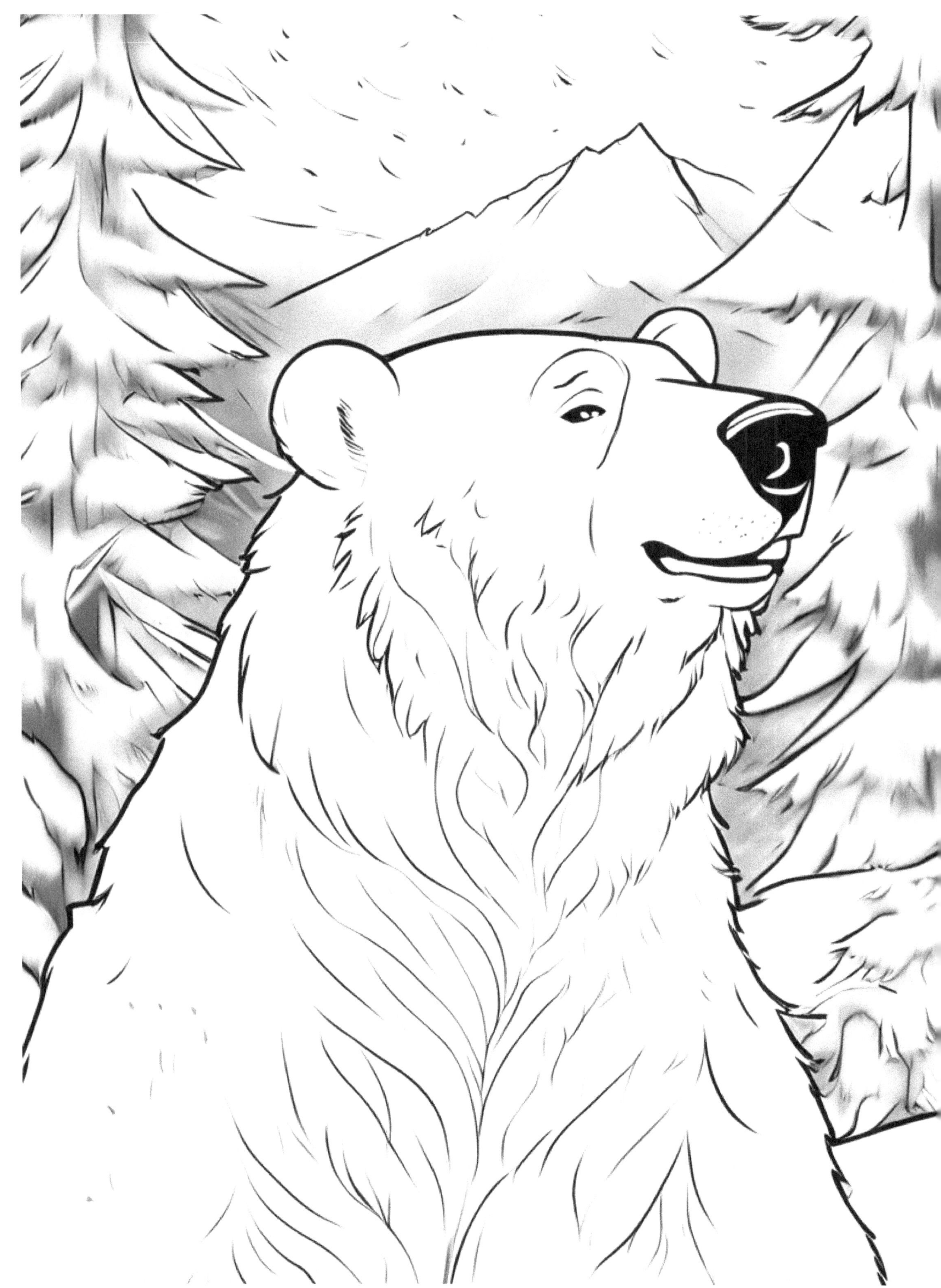